M

David Eldridge

methuen | drama
LONDON · NEW YORK · OXFORD · NEW DELHI · SYDNEY

METHUEN DRAMA
Bloomsbury Publishing Plc
50 Bedford Square, London, WC1B 3DP, UK
1385 Broadway, New York, NY 10018, USA
29 Earlsfort Terrace, Dublin 2, Ireland

BLOOMSBURY, METHUEN DRAMA and the Methuen Drama logo are trademarks of Bloomsbury Publishing Plc

First published in Great Britain 2022
Reprinted 2022

Cover design by National Theatre Graphic Design Studio

Cover image (Claire Rushbrook and Daniel Ryan) © David Stewart, 2022

A catalogue record for this book is available from the British Library.

A catalog record for this book is available from the Library of Congress

ISBN: PB: 978-1-3503-3440-3
ePDF: 978-1-3503-3441-0
eBook: 978-1-3503-3442-7

Series: Modern Plays

Typeset by Mark Heslington Ltd, Scarborough, North Yorkshire
Printed and bound in Great Britain

Middle had its premiere in the Dorfman theatre at the National Theatre, London, on 4 May 2022 with the following cast and creative team:

Maggie	**Claire Rushbrook**
Gary	**Daniel Ryan**
Director	**Polly Findlay**
Set and Costume Designer	**Fly Davis**
Lighting Designer	**Rick Fisher**
Sound Designer	**Donato Wharton**
Movement Director	**Anna Morrissey**
Fight Director	**Bret Yount**
Voice and Dialect Coach	**Nia Lynn**
Staff Director	**Lucy Jane Atkinson**

Middle

'Marriage is the waste-paper basket of the emotions.'
Sidney Webb, attributed by Beatrice Webb;
Bertrand Russell, 'Portraits from Memory' (1956)

'This is my lover's prayer
I hope it'll reach out to you, my love
This is my lover's prayer
And I hope you can understand it, my love'
Otis Redding, 'My Lover's Prayer' (1966)

'Every now and then I would feel a violent stab of loneliness. The very water I drink, the very air I breathe, would feel like long, sharp needles. The pages of a book in my hands would take on the threatening metallic gleam of razor blades. I could hear the roots of loneliness creeping through me when the world was hushed at four o'clock in the morning.'
Haruki Murakami, translated by Jay Rubin,
The Wind-Up Bird Chronicle (1997)

For Bertie, Wilf and George

Characters

Maggie
Gary

The play takes place in a real room and in real time – but stage directions are indicative, not prescriptive.

This play is the second of a loose trilogy of plays, or triptych for the theatre.

Thanks to Caroline Winder, Michael McCoy, Polly Findlay and Robert Holman.

Late February 2016.

The large kitchen of a detached house in Shenfield, Essex.

It's big enough to comfortably home a kitchen island with bar-stool-type chairs. It's spotlessly organised and clean but you can tell a child, or children, live in this house from some artwork on the fridge door.

The kitchen is mostly modern but there is a sideboard with glass cupboard doors containing their large collection of fine bone china tableware and dinnerware. Most stuff is put away leaving clean surfaces and lines. But there's a knife block. A Bluetooth speaker. And a fruit bowl with bananas, some satsumas and a couple of kiwi fruit.

Its neither night, nor morning, some time after 4 a.m. The only light is coming from the cooker hood and a lamp.

Maggie, *forty-nine, pours some milk into a saucepan and heats it on the hob. She does it carefully, slowly, she doesn't want to burn the milk, minding her dressing-gown sleeves. She glances briefly at her iPhone and then puts it in her dressing-gown pocket.*

In the kitchen doorway is her husband **Gary**, *forty-nine, in West Ham United pyjamas. He sips water that he brought down with him.*

He watches his wife pour the milk into her 'M' mug. She takes a sip. She finally looks at him.

They look at each other for a long time, for as long as you think you can get away with.

Gary Didn't you want to use the microwave?

Maggie No.

Gary It's a lot easier.

Maggie I didn't want to.

Gary Two minutes. Bing.

Silence.

Maggie I can never get it just how I want it.

Silence.

Gary Or put it on for a minute. Stick your finger in. Twenty more seconds. Thirty more seconds. Job done. Bosh.

Silence.

Maggie I would have thought a microwave's more of a 'bing' than a 'bosh'?

She smiles, sips. Silence.

Gary *comes further into the kitchen and slips his iPhone from his pyjama shorts pocket, looks at something and scrolls for a moment. Then he plugs it into a charger plugged into the wall. Silence.*

Gary What's wrong?

Silence.

Maggie I can't sleep. I haven't been to sleep at all.

Silence.

Gary What's wrong?

Silence.

Maggie I'm not sure I love you any more.

Gary *blinks and fetches the kettle which he fills and then flicks on.*

He fetches his 'G' mug and another fresh mug for **Maggie**.

He fetches the teapot from the sideboard. He watches the kettle boil. The kettle boils.

Gary Oh. You don't want any tea do you?

Maggie No.

He looks at her, composes himself. She looks at him, holds his gaze. Silence.

Gary What?

Silence.

Maggie Did you hear what I said?

Silence.

Gary You know what? We didn't defrost the pork.

He goes to the freezer and takes out a frozen pork belly.

I knew when we went to bed we'd forgotten something.

He finds a plate and puts the pork on it.

Maggie Gary, did you hear what I said?

Gary I know I'm in trouble when I'm 'Gary'.

He goes back to the mugs and teapot and throws in two teabags. He re-boils the kettle, pours water into the teapot. He looks at her.

Gary What?

Maggie Gary?

Gary I can't believe you woke me up again.

Silence.

I was having a really good sleep. I was in a really deep sleep. I was having a wonderful dream.

Silence.

I was in a big holiday camp. At a school reunion. Like that Butlin's at Minehead. But more old-fashioned, like *Hi-De-Hi!*. There was cod, chips and mushy peas for breakfast. All over that. And they was all there from school. But everyone had gone grey. Like exaggerated. Lucy Wilson looked like she had a silver wig on. And she was the fittest girl in my year. Adam Phillips had brought along the model he did of the Thames Barrier. As his geography project. And everyone said he was still a muppet. And Michael Keeley was taking pictures on a proper camera. We went on the flumes. Played on the penny pushers. Every one tried to crack on with Lucy Wilson like they did at school.

And she kept winking at me. But I ignored her. Everyone was dancing to 'So Macho'. By Sinitta. And we was all having a right laugh. Hands in the air. Like you just don't care.

Maggie I wish I had your dreams.

Silence.

There's never any point to them.

Gary They're just dreams.

Maggie I wish mine were like that.

Silence.

What was the one the other day?

Gary I dunno.

Maggie The one about the fish?

Gary The fishing one, the one at the fish counter in Sainsbury's, or the one about the funny smell in the lift at work?

Maggie What's the one about the funny smell in the lift at work?

Gary Didn't I tell you that one?

Maggie What's that one?

Gary It was an odd one. I had this dream. Just before I woke up. I was in the lift at work. And I went up in it. But I was on edge. And I didn't know why. I thought I could smell fish. So I didn't get out at my floor. And I went down again. And I went up and down about ten times. I was so on edge. I thought, I swear on my life I can smell haddock. I can really smell haddock. Then there was a horrendous noise. I thought I was having a heart attack! The alarm went off!

Maggie The fire alarm?

Gary No, my alarm! My real alarm! Did my nut right in. It was like I was in a hundred-piece puzzle. With eighty-two of the pieces missing. And to make it worse when I got in the actual lift at work. Like, the real, actual lift. It didn't smell of anything! And I even asked Johnny Cartwright if he could smell anything. And he looked at me like I'd confirmed once and for all I'm a liability. Everyone thinks I'm a liability at my firm.

Maggie *smiles and nods. Silence.*

Maggie I suppose that's the difference between real life and a dream. One's real and one's not.

Until it all starts to merge into the same thing.

Silence.

Gary So what was the one the other day about the fish?

Maggie Gary . . .

Gary Was it the one about the humungous carp?

Maggie I want to talk . . .

Gary Was it that one?

Maggie I've not slept for weeks.

Gary Just tell me. . .

Silence.

I know what this is all about. It was the same with me mum.

Silence.

Maggie What?

Gary The painters are no longer in very often. And in fact they're packing up. And they've nearly left the building.

Silence.

Maggie It's not that.

Silence.

You think this is about that?

Gary *moves as if in response to something he can hear upstairs.*

Gary That's Annabelle.

Maggie It's not.

Gary It is. That's Annabelle.

Maggie It's the radiator. At the top of the stairs.

Gary It's not.

Maggie The heating's come on.

Gary Are you cold?

Maggie No. Are you?

Gary I'm alright.

Maggie Why don't you go and put your hoodie on?

Gary I'm alright.

Maggie You're cold, I can see you're cold.

Gary I don't want to.

Silence.

Maggie She's never up in the night. You know she's not.

Silence.

She's not been up in the night since she was in reception.

Gary I was just saying . . .

Maggie Why don't you go and get your hoodie and have a peek in?

Gary I'm fine.

Maggie You'll reassure yourself.

Gary I'm alright as it is.

Maggie Go on.

Gary I don't want to.

Maggie I don't want you to be cold.

Gary It'll warm up.

Maggie I don't want you to worry.

Gary I know, it's the radiator.

Maggie I want us to talk. I don't want you to keep diverting off.

Gary I'm not.

Maggie You are.

Gary People say stuff when they're married. Truly awful terrible things. Things they don't mean.

Maggie Gary . . .

Gary I have . . .

Maggie Gary.

Gary I've said things to you . . .

Maggie Babe . . .

Gary That argument we had on holiday still brings me out in a cold sweat . . .

Maggie Gary, we don't need to go over it . . .

Gary What's with all the 'Gary'?

Maggie I just called you babe . . .

Gary Gary this, Gary that. Gary, Gary, Gary.

Silence.

Maggie Please. I want you to listen to me.

Gary I am, I swear.

Maggie I want you to pay attention.

Gary I'm all ears.

Maggie This is important.

Gary I know, babe.

Maggie Please help me.

Gary I want to.

Maggie Help me to do this well.

Gary Okay, okay . . .

Maggie I've wanted us to talk for weeks and weeks and weeks . . .

Gary I'm all ears, honest . . .

Maggie But since Friday . . .

Gary What happened Friday?

Maggie *cracks a touch, wipes away a couple of tears. Holds it together.*

Gary *goes to her, tries to hold her but she doesn't want him to. She pushes him away. Silence.*

Gary Mag . . . Honest, I'm all ears.

Maggie *looks at him. Silence.*

Gary*'s a little at a loss. He sips the water he brought down with him. He notices the pork belly on the plate.*

Gary What d'you think about sprinkling a few fennel seeds on that pork?

Maggie What?

Gary I had a little looky-see on tinterweb last night. And this one recipe reckons a rub. Fennel seeds, some chopped rosemary and lemon zest. With the seasoning and . . . Have we got any fennel seeds?

Maggie I've no idea.

Gary *looks about him, wanders a bit in the kitchen. Silence.*

Gary I love it in here. I love it, I just love it. Get the tunes going. The Roses, the Mondays, bit of Pulp. Bit of eighties. Bit of Prince. An old school banger. And indie banger. Bit of Luther. Bit of Otis.

Silence.

Rattle a few saucepans. Cook up a storm. You and me and Annabelle having a nice early dinner. A spag bol. A nice authentic one. Having a laugh.

Maggie I know.

Silence.

Gary You know if you're not up to Mum and Dad . . .

Maggie I'm not sure I am . . .

Gary I mean we made such a song and dance. About saying thank you for last weekend . . . And Annabelle's gonna be like: 'What's happened to Nanny and Grandad?'

Maggie I don't even know where I'm gonna be in the next ten minutes. Let alone this afternoon.

Silence.

Gary D'you want a brandy?

Maggie No.

Gary You sure?

Maggie Yep.

Gary I think there's a Baileys left over from Christmas . . .

Maggie I don't want a drink.

Gary It might help . . .

Maggie It won't. . .

Gary I might still have that spliff that Spam Face gave me on my forty-fifth. I think it's in me pant drawer . . .

Maggie Gary . . .

Gary Might be a bit. . .

He smacks his lips and waggles his tongue.

Maggie I don't want to drink, I don't want to get stoned. I want to talk.

Silence.

Gary Alright.

Silence.

We had a lovely Valentine's weekend away. Lovely. Didn't we? Lovely pub, lovely grub, nice walk on the beach. Lovely room. Sex twice. Twice

Maggie I know.

Silence.

Gary It was great to get away on our own.

Silence.

Maggie I didn't want to.

Gary Go away?

Maggie Have sex with you.

Silence.

Gary Mag? What you saying, Mag?

Maggie I haven't wanted to have sex with you for ages.

Silence.

But I've done it. I've done it. I have done. I read up, I talk to people, I'm not stupid.

Things change. Things can change. But you think of your marriage. Get the lube out. 'It's like having a biscuit. Once you've had one, you feel like another one.' Why do you think I've done it? Why d'you think we did it twice?

She wipes away a few tears, then composes herself. Silence.

Gary Don't you fancy me no more?

Silence.

Maggie I wish we were healthier. But I'm the same. It's hard working up town. How many times have I tried to have that conversation with you, Gary?

Silence.

Maggie I think there's things we could have done.

Silence.

Gary Annabelle's school fees ain't gonna pay for themselves are they, Mag? I ain't gonna be able to do what we need to driving an Uber am I?

Maggie Sending her to a prep school was your choice.

Silence.

Gary Look, I feel gutted, right.

Maggie I'm sorry.

Silence.

Gary It's gonna go up and down ain't it, babe?

Maggie What is?

Gary We've had our ups and downs. Like everyone.

Maggie What are you talking about, Gary?

Gary You know, the fancying. Even when you've hit the jackpot and married an Adonis like me.

He makes a few shapes to try and make **Maggie** *laugh. He has no luck. Silence.*

Maggie Gary . . .

Gary We ain't had no time for ourselves for donkey's years. Listen to me . . .

Maggie No, Gary, listen to me . . . Please.

Gary My opinion on this, right. You've got to tackle these things. Head on. You've almost got to have a hit list . . . In the sack.

Maggie No, Gary . . .

Gary Stay with me, babe.

Maggie No, I don't want to . . .

Gary I think with the sex thing. There's bits and bobs we can do . . .

Maggie Bits and bobs?

Gary Yeah.

Hearing him talk like this is very hard for her. Silence.

C'mon! We can jazz things up!

Maggie *looks at the clock on the wall, nearer five than four now.*

Gary When it comes to the bedroom department, I may not always be Uri Geller. But I have on occasion unwittingly stumbled upon your internet history. Forgive me. But who am I to quibble, if two big hairy coppers with leather chaps and a multifunctional truncheon are forming a queue at Mrs Maggie's Wank Bank?

He holds his hands up.

Maggie No, Gary, I . . .

Gary I ain't never gonna be the most hirsute fella, babe. But as for the attire. They do next-day delivery at 'Love Your Leather dot co dot UK'.

He smiles.

We've all got fantasies. I have. I can tell you. I'm in a black cab. Going down a country lane on a hot summer's day. I'm sweaty. And my driver. She's sweaty. If you want me to paint a picture. She's like Carole Kirkwood's younger sister. Just less smiley. Almost sullen. Like she needs me to take her away from all this. And I can just see a little bit of boob . . . In the rear-view mirror. And I'm like, 'Hello, soldier.' And I say to her, 'You look like you need cheering up darling.'

Maggie *puts her head in her hands. Silence.*

Gary I bought you a vibrator.

Maggie You didn't, did you?

Gary Surprise!

Silence.

Well, I wanted it to be a surprise. I was gonna bring it last weekend. But you kept coming in when I was packing my bag. And then Annabelle was in and out with her iPad.

Maggie Oh God . . .

Gary I wanted you to feel nice. I was nervous.

Silence.

And like I wanted you to know. I didn't take you for granted. And I was really cacking my pants buying it. I put me Peaky Blinder on and me Ray-Bans on when I went in Ann Summers in Romford.

Maggie *covers her mouth with her hands, eyes still closed, finding courage.*

Gary I reckon I went in and out of there about ten times before I had the nerve to pick one up. And I didn't know whether you might want like a. Cool midget-type one. Or a great big donger . . .

Maggie Gary . . .

Silence.

Gary In the end I just bought one of each. Fuck it.

Silence.

The big lad's a nine-inch throbbing veined monster. Made with hospital-grade silicone.

I've hid him in the loft. He's in with the Christmas decorations.

Silence.

Maggie I don't love you any more. It doesn't matter how much you talk and talk and talk. I don't love you any more.

Gary Stop it.

Silence.

Maggie I don't love you any more.

Gary Stop it.

Maggie I don't, I don't love you any more.

Gary Stop it.

Maggie I don't love you any more.

Gary Mag, darling . . .

Maggie I don't love you any more.

Gary Mag . . .

Maggie I wanted to talk to you. But I knew it would be like this. I'm just going to go upstairs and get a few things and go to Mum's. I don't want a scene with Annabelle. You can make up whatever excuse you like. And perhaps once you're in the frame of mind to talk. Then we can talk.

Gary *blinks away a tear, cut to the core. Silence.*

Maggie Are you crying?

Gary No.

Maggie I don't mind.

Gary I'm not.

They look at each other for a long time, for as long as you think you can get away with.

Maggie Do you want a brandy?

Gary No.

Maggie It might help.

Gary I'm alright.

Maggie Limoncello?

Gary I don't think now's the moment for a limoncello.

Maggie Go on.

Gary I tend to associate a limoncello with a nice meal at Tarantino's.

Silence.

Or the lovely holiday we had in Italy.

Silence.

Maggie Why don't you have a brandy?

Gary I can't . . .

Maggie Why not?

Gary I've got to take Annabelle football.

Maggie Not until nine . . .

Gary No . . .

Maggie Maybe she won't go football tomorrow for once . . .

Gary It's already today.

Maggie Maybe she won't go football today . . .

Gary No she's not missing it . . .

Maggie Why not?

Gary Because we've got Great Danes away. And when we played them on Remembrance Sunday that little redhead one didn't half send Annabelle up in the air. So tomorrow Annabelle is gonna kick that little shit into the back of her own net.

Maggie Gary . . .

Gary We've discussed it, babe. 'The Terminator' has been mentioned.

Maggie What?

Gary Julian Dicks. 'The Terminator'. We've been on YouTube and had a look at the two-footed 'Dennis Wise' that got him his first straight red . . .

Maggie You haven't?

Gary Course I haven't. She's eight.

Silence.

Why don't you love me no more?

Silence.

Maggie I do. As a friend.

Gary As a friend?

Silence.

Sixteen years and I'm in the friend zone?

Silence.

Why don't you love me no more?

Silence.

Maggie We are friends . . . And we're family. And we're parents . . .

Gary Like, I know you're more intelligent than me . . .

Maggie Don't say that . . .

Gary You are . . .

Maggie Well, I'm not . . .

Gary But I'm not thick.

Maggie I know you're not.

Gary Brian next door. Now he's thick . . .

Maggie What's this got to do with Brian?

Gary I'm not thick . . .

Maggie I know you're not.

Gary Then when I ask you a straight question why won't you answer it?

Silence.

Maggie Because I'm frightened. I'm petrified.

Gary Of me?

Maggie No.

Gary What?

Maggie Can't you understand why I'm scared?

Gary You're scared? And how d'you think I'm feeling right now?

Silence.

I've only got up for a piss. And you're insomniac again. Up and down. Rolling over this way, rolling over that way. Crying.

Maggie If you knew I was crying why didn't you say something?

Gary Why do you think?

Maggie Why didn't you give me a cuddle?

Gary Because I'm shitting myself that's why! I'm frightened half to death!

Silence.

Maggie I honestly don't know where to start.

Gary You've already started.

Maggie It's hard.

She walks in the kitchen, trying to be composed and find courage. Silence.

I'm so bored.

Silence.

I feel so lonely.

Silence.

I'm so sorry to hurt you like this, Gary.

She wants to cry but maintains her composure. **Gary** *is devastated. Silence.*

Maggie Let me try and do this as best I can.

Silence.

Remember when we first met? It was the first Friday back after Millennium Eve right?

Gary I know when it was.

Maggie In Hamilton Hall.

Gary I know where it was.

Maggie There's something I never told you.

Silence.

I bumped into my ex.

Gary In Hamilton Hall?

Maggie On Bishopsgate.

Gary Outside the pub?

Maggie Outside The Woodins Shades.

Gary You said . . .

Maggie I know what I said.

Gary You said you just fancied a drink before you got on the train?

Maggie I did.

Gary You didn't do anything did you?

Maggie What d'you mean?

Gary With him . . .

Maggie Like what?

Gary Before you met me?

Maggie I bumped into him on the street outside The Woodins Shades!

Silence.

Gary Well, what then?

Silence.

Maggie He told me it was biggest mistake of his life letting me go. He had tears in his eyes. He was always a man who had tears in his eyes when he needed them.

Silence.

And as he waved his hands about. Declaring his love and asking me for my new number. I was crying. Because he hurt me so much. And deep down I still loved him. And I thought about him. And then I could see it glinting. His wedding ring. Waving his hands about, he was. 'I love you Maggie, I love you.' And it meant nothing more to him than a tinsel end in the gutter.

Silence.

Gary Your ex was married?

Silence.

Why didn't you tell me?

Maggie It didn't affect you . . .

Gary Didn't it?

Maggie I walked away from him. And I walked away from every shit-bag City boy I ever knew. With the gift of the gab, a pair of loafers and two nights a week in a titty bar. And you was there. You was at the bar.

She closes her eyes. Silence.

Gary You told me you'd had a crap day at work?

Maggie I had. And you said, 'Don't worry about it. Have a drink with me.' And you told me you'd look after me. That whatever happened you'd look after me. And you always have.

Silence.

Why do you think I've been breaking my heart in the middle of the night?

Silence.

I feel so shit.

Silence.

Gary You married me and you loved someone else?

Maggie I didn't love anyone else.

Gary Well, what you saying?

Maggie Look at me, you must believe me, I loved you.

Silence.

When we got together it was complicated for me . . .

Gary It wasn't complicated for me . . .

Maggie But it was for me.

Silence.

Gary I thought those were golden times . . .

Maggie They were!

Gary Don't sound like it . . .

Maggie They were!

Gary Sounds like it was a bit complicated for you . . .

Maggie You have this black and white view of things, Gary.

Silence.

I'm trying to be honest with you . . . It didn't affect you. I've never seen him or spoken to him since. Even if I've wondered from time to time. I've never enquired. I've never slid into his DMs. I've never done any social media stalking. The minute I met you he was already behind me . . .

Silence.

Gary Why are you bringing all this up?

Silence.

Can you explain something to me?

Maggie I'll try . . .

Gary I've never understood it.

Maggie Okay . . .

Gary What's sliding into your DMs?

Maggie *smiles. Silence.*

Gary Honest . . . Is it like . . . Like standing in someone else's shoes?

Maggie That's lovely.

Gary Is it though?

Maggie No.

Gary Tell me.

Maggie It's sending a private message on social media.

Gary Oh . . . that's what it's called!

He becomes sheepish. Silence.

Maggie I was heartbroken and you fixed me.

Silence.

Gary Why are you bringing all this up?

Silence.

Maggie There were golden times. Our honeymoon in Krabi was like a dream. I'll remember the day we spent in Phang Nga Bay until the day I die. I've never had such a laugh. I've never felt so safe with a bloke. They were golden times. They were. It was such a good time.

We were always having a laugh. And we had such nice sex. Sexy sex.

Silence.

When you asked me to marry you I knew it was me and you forever. I knew.

Gary Why don't you love me any more?

Silence.

Maggie You made me want things I never wanted before. I wanted a big house on the Mount. I wanted big holidays. Dubai. The Maldives. Tahiti. I wanted a family.

Gary I know you wasn't sure about having Annabelle . . .

Maggie That's not true . . .

Gary Be honest.

Silence.

Maggie I was never the one who needed to have a kid as soon I could. That's all. Annabelle's my world. She's our world. How can you say that? I'm different to you, Gary. Jesus Christ, we're sixteen years down the road and you still don't get me? Why do you think we're having this conversation? Why?

Silence.

I find Annabelle difficult.

Gary She's alright.

Maggie Well, maybe you think she's alright because she's not difficult with you.

Gary She can be.

Maggie She's always been Daddy's girl.

Silence.

I was stuck with her all the time.

Gary Stuck with her?

Maggie That's how it felt.

Silence.

Gary You know there's women who'd be grateful to be in that position . . .

Maggie I know. But I'm me. And I wanted a year out. Max.

Silence.

Gary We was gonna try for another one.

Maggie I didn't want to have another one.

Gary But you promised me we'd try for another one.

Maggie No, Gary, I promised to keep an open mind . . .

Gary Well, maybe we should have had a shag once in a while. Or you should have kept our appointment . . .

Maggie I was all over the place. I'm sorry.

Gary And I was up and down Harley Street like some wally who'd gone to the wrong clinic . . .

Maggie I'm sorry, I've said I'm sorry a hundred times.

Silence.

I didn't always have luck with men. But I had a great life. And then I spent five years on my own.

Gary Don't be silly . . .

Maggie I'm not. Five years on my own . . .

Gary You weren't on your own . . .

Maggie You're out the door at six every morning. You're out up town three nights a week. Your clients tell you to bend over, you bend over. I mean who goes on a client's stag do?

You're playing golf, you're over West Ham . . . You're forty-nine years of age. Where's it all going to end? When you drop down dead of a heart attack?

Silence.

My mum told me, when you have a kid you just have to accept your relationship plateaus for a while. Or it goes backwards. Well, there's that and there's your marriage falling off of Beachy Head. Except when it's smashed to bits on the rocks. It refuses to die. It's just stuck there, bored and tired and lonely. Trying to attract some attention. Someone. Anyone. Help me. The tide goes in, the tide goes out. Still there. No one notices, no one cares. Bleeding to death for eternity.

Silence.

Gary Everyone finds having a kid hard.

Maggie There's hard and there's hard . . .

Gary Things have been fine since you've been back at work . . .

Maggie Things have been tolerable. That's not the same . . .

Gary Come on, Mag, what is this bullshit?

Maggie Believe you me, I've been circumspect. I'll tell you another thing you didn't know. If you didn't let me go back to work when Annabelle started school I was going.

Gary Let you go back to work?

Maggie You heard me . . .

Gary You do as you please, babe . . .

Maggie You heard me . . .

Gary Going where?

Maggie I was leaving.

Gary Well, perhaps you should have done and saved yourself another three years of misery with me?

Maggie I often wish I did.

Gary *paces; this is all so hard. Silence.*

Maggie You have no idea how patient I've been.

Gary Why are you bringing all this shit up from years ago?

Silence.

I don't want this.

Maggie I didn't want us to argue . . .

Gary I love you.

Silence.

Maggie I wanted to talk. And explain how I feel in an honest, calm way. I've been going over it and over it in my mind.

Silence.

Gary And what about my feelings? Don't I have feelings? Or am I just the geezer?

Maggie I'm sorry I've hurt you . . . I am.

Gary Hurt me? You've cut me in half.

Silence.

Maggie I've always thought about you.

Gary Have you?

Maggie When I first met you it was complicated. Of course, I thought about whether I was being fair. Of course, I felt guilty. Like I was carrying around unfinished business. But I really liked you. And I fell in love with you.

Silence.

It was right giving things between us a chance. I was so happy. Those years were great. I loved our wedding. Loved it. All the dancing. The eighties theme. The silly dancing. To Yazz. And Bros. And Wham.

Silence.

I never dreamed it would take so long to have Annabelle. I just didn't.

Silence.

I always thought it would be so smooth. I was so terrified by my mum growing up. Use contraception or you'll get pregnant. So obviously I thought as soon as we start trying it'll happen.

Silence.

Like I know how normal losing a pregnancy is now. Losing a baby. A little baby. Can be. But it wasn't normal to me. It was devastating. It happening. And then again. And the IVF not working out. That was really hard. Depressing. And. Like it made me feel we weren't meant to be. Somehow. Like on some deep level of fate. It completely doomed us.

Silence.

And when I fell pregnant with Annabelle I . . . And it just happened. Naturally. Like it was supposed to all along. It wasn't just like it was a miracle. It was confirmation. Like we were all right with the world. We were meant to be.

Silence.

I was so ecstatic I . . . I was like. This is our dream. This is our dream come true. This is it. And then when she was here.

Gary She was a miracle.

Silence.

You had a fortnight off work. And it was a blur. I can't really remember it. And then you went back to work. And I was on my own.

Silence.

I spent a lot of time feeling guilty. Not at first. But once we were married and trying to have a family.

Silence.

I felt like I was letting you down. Letting Annabelle down.

Silence.

And when I couldn't breast-feed I felt like a complete failure. I felt worse than you can possibly imagine. I don't think we ever talked about it once. Not even once.

Silence.

And when you went back to work. Annabelle was two weeks old. I was so scared, and so lonely and isolated . . .

Gary You had your mates . . .

Maggie Thank God. Thank God.

Silence.

Five years of mums. Mum-ness. I've written the book, got the badge. There's not a children's entertainer in Essex I'm not on first-name terms with. Awesome Andrew sends me a personalised e-Christmas card . . .

Gary Who's he?

Maggie Did the kite-flying party for Annabelle's fourth birthday. In Weald Park. I advised Jill at Stay and Play on improving her range of healthy snacks. For children. And adults. I made and consumed every possible variety and concoction of cupcake. My chocolate and salted caramel ones with a Rolo were a hit for two years running. And my pistachio with hand-crafted mermaid tails were spectacular. I even did the crab apple cider ones for the adults last year. But no one ate them. And that twat who thinks she's Jordan with a tit job, four feral kids and twenty-two-year-old boyfriend complained we'd run out of Prosecco.

Silence.

Yeah I had my mates. To laugh and cry with. Thank God. But I needed you.

Silence.

And I even felt guilty for needing you so much. Because I thought he's paying for all this. This massive house. Everything. And I felt bad even for thinking. Surely we can get a babysitter? And not rely on my lot. Or your lot. So we can go out and do stuff on our own. And it be just us. And not tell anyone. Do whatever we like. And then I'm feeling bad. Because then I'm thinking he works so hard. He's out so much with work. When he's home, he just wants to be home.

Silence.

I love being a mum. I love it. It's hard, it's fucking hard. But I was so much more than that. I am so much more than that. A mum. And a wife.

Silence.

Believe me, I've been circumspect. Rattling around in a big empty house. It's been better in the last few years since I've been back to work but . . .

Silence.

I really appreciate everything you do for us. I really do. But what about me?

Silence.

You wanted another one. But I always had two children to look after.

Silence.

I reckon you're right. I reckon I'm perimenopausal. I've been to the doctor.

Silence.

I know I'm getting on. And as I'm thinking about getting older. I'm frightened.

Silence.

The thought of us being together. Getting old together. It used to make me feel so safe.

Gary *starts to wipe away a few tears. Silence.*

Maggie I'm sorry.

Gary What for?

Maggie Let me get you a tissue . . .

Gary I don't need a tissue.

Maggie Gary . . .

Gary I told you, Mag. That floor cleaner you use in here makes my eyes itch. When Annabelle makes a mess use the Mr Muscle Five-in-One.

Silence.

Why are you doing this?

Silence.

Funnily enough five years of endometriosis and my below-par sperm count wasn't on my bucket list. But you wanted to be at home with Annabelle . . .

Maggie Not forever.

Gary It wasn't forever . . .

Maggie It felt like it. I didn't want everything to be on my shoulders . . .

Gary You've got a short memory . . .

Maggie I didn't put my hand up for that.

Gary Tell me what to do.

Maggie What?

Gary Tell me what to do. To put things right.

Maggie Gary . . .

Gary I love you, Mag. I've loved you since the minute I set eyes on you.

Maggie Gary, please . . .

Gary You know it's true.

Maggie Please just let's talk.

Gary You tell me what to do and I'll do it, babe.

Silence.

I thought all this was water well under the bridge. As it goes, since Annabelle started school. And you went back to work. I thought things had been great. I think things have been weird. Like lately. I thought you was a bit quiet over Christmas. And off like a rocket. But I thought, she's just starting to go through the change. We had such a lovely Valentine's last weekend. Didn't we?

Silence.

When you told me you didn't want another kid. And you wanted to go back to work. I was gutted. But I accepted it. And I did what you want. Because that's what you do, right? When you're married and you love someone. Right? But that's three years ago now, darling. We're plodding along. Annabelle's thriving. We have a couple of nice holidays a year. We get out. Maybe not as often we should. But we get a nice date night. My lot help out. Or your lot. Annabelle's getting bigger. Perhaps we should have more nights away.

He studies her. Silence.

You tell me. Tell me what you want and I'll do it.
I promise you.

Maggie *thinks, finds courage, walks in the kitchen.* **Gary** *watches her. Silence.*

Maggie I think I'm in love with someone else.

Gary *is shattered. Silence.*

Maggie I'm sorry. I'm so sorry.

Silence.

Gary Who? Is it your ex?

Maggie Gary . . .

Gary Is he back on the scene?

Maggie No.

Silence.

Gary Is it Martin?

Maggie No, of course it's not.

Gary Who is it?

Maggie It's not Martin. It's no one at work.

Silence.

Gary Who is it then?

Silence.

Maggie His name's John.

Gary John?

Maggie Yeah.

Gary I don't know any John.

Maggie I know you don't.

Gary There's John down the road. But he's eighty-two and he's deaf as a post.

Silence.

Maggie You don't know him.

Silence.

Gary You've been having an affair?

Maggie I haven't slept with him.

Silence.

Gary You haven't shagged him?

Maggie No.

Gary I don't understand this.

Silence.

Maggie I feel so awful.

Gary You haven't shagged him?

Maggie No.

Gary I don't . . .

Maggie But when I saw him on Friday . . .

Gary On Friday?

Maggie At lunchtime.

Gary Lunchtime?

Maggie We meet for a Pret. Or sometimes YO! Sushi.

Gary YO! Sushi?

Maggie Yeah.

Gary I thought you didn't like sushi?

Maggie Well, you know . . . I've given it a go.

Silence.

When I saw John on Friday we kissed.

Gary You kissed another man?

Maggie Passionately.

Gary *weeps a bit, wipes away a few tears, holds it together. Silence.*

Maggie And I felt like a Rubicon had been crossed.

Silence.

It's a saying . . .

Gary I know what crossing the Rubicon means.

Silence.

Maggie I'm sorry.

Gary I know I didn't go to uni like you . . .

Maggie I didn't mean to patronise you . . .

Gary You never do.

Silence.

Maggie I'm sorry I've hurt you . . .

Gary I'm alright . . .

Maggie Let me get you some kitchen roll . . .

Gary I've told you already, I'm not crying . . .

Maggie You don't have to pretend to . . .

Gary If I was crying don't you think I'd know about it?

Silence.

Maggie Okay, Gary, alright.

Gary John?

Maggie Yeah.

Gary What's John do then?

Maggie He's a policeman.

Gary *sits down and puts his head in his hands. Silence.*

Maggie He's not like a uniformed policeman. He hasn't got a truncheon. They were phased out in the mid-nineties. John explained. Like, I have seen a picture of him in his dress uniform. When he was younger. But he's a detective. You know Brian next door has actually got criminal associations. John's in Homicide and Major Crime Command. He's a very impressive man.

Silence.

I met him in the pub. Much like I met you.

Silence.

Gary Is John married as well?

Maggie It's on its last legs.

Gary What is?

Maggie His marriage.

Gary Right.

Maggie He's not loved his wife for years.

Silence.

He's been a very good friend over the last three months.

Gary Three months?

Silence.

Maggie I won't lie. We've both felt tempted. But we've kept each other on the straight and narrow.

Silence.

Gary So what's been going on?

Maggie It's all been very innocent.

Gary It doesn't sound innocent to me.

Maggie I feel so shit.

Silence.

Gary Don't you think you owe me an explanation?

Maggie *nods. Silence.*

Gary You met him in a pub?

Maggie Yeah.

Gary Where?

Maggie Does it matter?

Gary Before Christmas?

Maggie More like November.

Silence.

I met him in Dirty Dicks.

Gary Dirty Dicks?

Maggie On Bishopsgate.

Gary I am familiar with the establishment.

Maggie Alright.

Gary Was it that leaving do? Was it? Ella's leaving do?

Maggie *nods. Silence.*

Maggie He chatted me up at the bar.

Gary Chatted you up?

Maggie Well, not chatted up, chatted up . . . It wasn't like that. He told me all about his wife. And his kids.

Gary He's got kids as well has he?

Maggie He was just being friendly. I told you. It was all very innocent.

Silence.

He found me on Facebook . . .

Gary He's not on your Facebook is he?

Maggie No!

Gary Our whole life's on Facebook!

Silence.

Maggie It's not Gary, is it?

Silence.

I've kept him completely out of our life.

Silence.

We just struck up a private friendship. He's having a really hard time. I feel so sorry for him. His eldest daughter from his first marriage is anorexic and his wife's got an over-active thyroid.

Silence.

I was lonely. I am lonely. You've got no idea. I can't sleep. I'm awake. I know you're awake as well. Neither of us is saying nothing. And sometimes my heart. It's like it hurts so much. It's so swollen. Like it could burst. And then, then. It's like it's being squeezed. And squeezed. Like it's in the grip of something terrible. And unyielding. And I feel like I can hardly breathe.

Silence.

It's got a hold of me night and day. Night and day. Night time is worst. I never dreamed in all my life my marriage bed could be so lonely.

Silence.

It's taken me a long time to realise how lonely I've been, Gary. Because you to tend to think. When people say they're lonely. You tend to think of solitude. Of being on your own. But it's a different kind of loneliness. All the things you want to say but you can't. The sadness of it. The disappointment.

Silence.

I know this is selfish. After everything I've said. But all I want you to do is cuddle me in the night. And kiss my ear. And tell me you'll look after me.

Silence.

But it's not fair is it.

Silence.

We've got a lot in common.

Gary Thank you.

Maggie I meant me and John.

Silence.

We come from very similar backgrounds. He's from Royal Tunbridge Wells. His dad was a civil servant and his mum was a teacher. Well, she's gone now but. And he went to university. And he got a job up town. He was a graduate in the Bank of England. But a desk job didn't suit him at all. And so he became a copper. He's like me. He's very interested in current affairs. And whatnot.

Silence.

And you know he says he likes nothing more. Nothing more. Than to listen to Classic FM and read a book. He reads everything that's on the shortlist for the William Hill Sports Book of the Year.

Silence.

And I think I'd like that. Instead of coming in and sticking the telly on. Whatever Annabelle's watching on Netflix. Or whatever you're watching on Sky Sports News. Listen to the radio. And read a book.

Silence.

I grew up in a house where Radio 4 was always on. When I was younger I always had my nose in a book. I don't know where she's gone.

Silence.

Or perhaps we could talk. Actually talk to each other.

Gary I thought we did.

Maggie We don't talk. We give each other instructions.We make arrangements.

Silence.

John's been a very good friend. Very good. When we meet up for a drink. Or a coffee. Or to go to an exhibition.

Gary You've been to an exhibition with him?

Maggie To the Tate Modern. I told you I've been wanting to go for ages.

Gary No you didn't.

Silence.

Maggie We talk. We talk and talk and talk and talk and talk and talk and talk and talk.

Silence.

Sometimes lately. I can get to thinking. Maybe I've met my soulmate.

Silence.

Maybe this is finally it.

Silence.

And more and more. I can't stop thinking about him.

Silence.

I just can't. From the minute I open my eyes. When I made the tea yesterday morning. I imagined making him tea. He likes it weak. I think it looks like cat's piss. But it's how he likes it. When I had my shower I thought about him . . . I.

Silence.

Until the minute I finally decided to come down. And make myself a drink. That's what it's been like. Since Friday. Since he give me a late Valentine's card. And he finally took my hand. And I let him kiss me.

Gary *stands.*

Gary You've made him tea?

Silence.

You've had him, haven't you? You're bullshitting me, this is all shit . . .

Maggie I haven't. I promise you. He came here one morning. When I had the day off to go to Thaxted. With Annabelle's school.

Gary What, so that was all lies?

Maggie It wasn't till the afternoon.

Silence.

John was impressed with your golf clubs.

Gary He what?

Maggie He liked your sand iron.

Gary He what?

Maggie He pulled it out and had a swing.

Gary He had a swing with my sand iron?

Silence.

Maggie John wanted to kiss me.

Gary You've brought this man into my home?

Maggie But I lost my nerve.

Gary You was gonna have some fucking bloke in our bed?

Maggie No . . .

Gary Oh, one of the guest bedrooms. That's alright then.

Maggie No, Gary, I wasn't.

Gary Well, what was he here for then?

Maggie I meant my marriage vows, Gary.

She lifts her left hand almost defiantly. **Gary** *looks at her, her wedding ring. She lets her hand fall. Silence.*

Maggie I've been thinking about when I met you a lot. I've not slept a wink. We was only thirty-three then.

Silence.

I was having an affair with a married man. It was over. I was heartbroken again. I was majorly on the rebound. I wanted security. I wanted someone nice for a change. And you was there.

Silence.

Then sixteen years later here I am. Again. I feel like things have come full circle.

Silence.

Sometimes I think I don't deserve you, Annabelle. All this. And sometimes I think I settled for someone and something I never should have. In a million years.

She studies **Gary**. *Silence.*

Maggie I want to be completely honest. That's all.

Gary *opens the sideboard cupboard doors and methodically smashes every single piece of tableware and dinnerware in there on the kitchen floor. It takes as long as it takes.*

Finally he comes across a surviving milk jug. He looks at it and then throws it as hard as he can across the room. **Maggie** *ducks, and it smashes against the opposite wall. Silence.*

Gary You know what . . .

Maggie What?

Gary It's overrated . . .

Maggie What is?

Gary Complete honesty.

He closes the sideboard cupboards and then punches the glass one on the upper right side.

He immediately howls with pain as the glass smashes and as he withdraws his right hand we can see it's cut. There's immediately blood running down his forearm, onto his pyjamas and dripping on to the floor.

Maggie *moves quickly for the first-aid box in one of the kitchen cupboards.* **Gary** *goes to the sink and runs his hand under the tap before elevating it. It's still bleeding.*

Maggie *approaches him but hesitates before touching him.*

He demurs and **Maggie** *opens the box and immediately sets about patching* **Gary** *up, drying his hand first and examining it.*

Maggie It's not as bad as it looks. But it might need a stitch.

Gary I'm not going up the hospital.

Maggie You might get a nasty scar.

Gary Something to remember tonight by.

Maggie Piss off, Gary.

They both hear something upstairs and freeze. Silence.

Gary That's Annabelle.

They listen for a bit and then **Maggie** *bolts to the kitchen doorway and looks down the hallway towards the bottom of the stairs waiting to see if she comes down.*

She makes a decision and disappears off for a moment.

Gary *feels sick and takes a breath and then another breath to calm himself. He goes to his iPhone in the wall, takes it, opens an app and begins scrolling through. Silence.* **Maggie** *re-enters.*

Maggie She'd gone to the toilet and gone back to bed.

She goes back to **Gary** *and re-takes his injured hand, a little blood seeping through the big plaster covering the cut. She binds his hand with some bandage.* **Gary** *looks at his iPhone in his free hand avoiding eye contact.*

Maggie *packs up the first-aid box and puts it back in the cupboard it came from. She looks at the mess, she looks at* **Gary**. *Silence.*

Maggie Let's just call it a day. I'll go to Mum's.

Gary *looks at her and then back at his iPhone.* **Maggie** *looks at* **Gary** *and all the mess in the kitchen. Silence.*

Maggie What did you do that for?

Gary What's the point . . .

Maggie What d'you mean what's the point?

Gary You're leaving us . . .

Maggie What?

Gary You're leaving me.

They look at each other for a long time, for as long as you think you can get away with.

I do take an interest in the news. Actually.

Maggie I know you do.

Gary *looks at his iPhone. Silence.*

Gary I do read the odd book. I've read Steven Gerrard's *My Story*. And I'm working myself up to *The Hairy Dieters*.

Maggie I know you do.

Silence.

We need to talk, Gary.

Gary Don't you think it's best in the morning, now? Let's just have a tidy-up. And I'll go in the spare room. Or you can. Whatever you want.

Maggie It is the morning.

Silence.

Gary Don't you think one of us should go up and see if Annabelle's alright?

Maggie You go . . .

Gary No . . .

Maggie Go on, you go, I'll clear up.

Gary No, you go . . .

Maggie Go on . . .

Gary It's my mess. I made the mess. I'll clear it up.

Maggie Why don't you make yourself a drink?

Gary Honestly . . .

Maggie Just sit down for five minutes. And when I come back down we can clean up together. And we can talk.

Gary *nods. They both hesitate, somehow not wanting to be apart from each other, even for a moment. Silence.*

Maggie *goes out again.*

Gary *looks about him at all the mess. He notices that the teapot survived as it was no longer in the sideboard.*

He glances at the knife block and on impulse takes the carving knife. He rests the blade against the artery in his neck and closes his eyes.

He rests the blade against his left wrist and then quite suddenly he begins to cry. It pours out of him, all of the agony of the moment. And then quite as suddenly he stops and pulls himself together. Puts the knife down on the island.

He goes to a long cupboard and retrieves a dustpan and brush and a hoover. He gets down on his knees with the dustpan and brush, beginning with the remains of the milk jug.

Maggie *comes in.* **Gary** *looks at her.*

Maggie She's sound asleep.

Gary That's good.

Maggie As I was looking at her . . . Our whole life together. It flashed before my eyes.

She starts to cry, great hulking sobs. She holds her arms out as if she wants **Gary** *to come and comfort her.*

Gary *hesitates, silence, save for the sound of her crying. Then he goes to her and holds her. They stand there holding each other, just holding each other, for as long as you think you can get away with.*

Maggie'*s upset and tears gradually fall away. Silence.*

She becomes self-conscious and breaks away from **Gary**, *wondering what she's doing, and heading for the hoover.*

Gary *watches her as she uncoils the lead, plugs it in and begins to hoover up quite blithely just ignoring the bits of china that are too big to be sucked up.*

Eventually she stops. **Gary** *is still watching her. She picks up the remainder of the milk jug* **Gary** *had before. Looks at it.*

Gary I wasn't aiming at you.

Maggie I wouldn't blame you if you were.

Gary It was just a . . .

Maggie I honestly wouldn't blame you if you were.

Gary Are you okay?

Maggie Been better.

Silence.

Are you okay?

Gary Been better.

He doesn't know what to say, so he begins to collect up by hand and with the dustpan the bigger bits of crockery.

Maggie *helps too. It all goes in the bin. Silence.*

Maggie I don't know what you must think of me.

Silence.

I mean . . . If it was you who got up in the middle of the night and said all this to me . . . I'd have already slung you out.

Silence.

Gary Do you want to leave?

Maggie Do you want me to leave?

Gary No.

Maggie Even after what I've said?

Gary No. I love you Maggie. I love you.

He retrieves his iPhone and goes to the Bluetooth speaker, which he switches on.

He quickly finds something on his iPhone and presses play. 'My Lover's Prayer' by Otis Redding plays.

Gary *sways in time to it, looking intently at* **Maggie**.

Maggie Turn it off, Gary.

Gary This is our song.

Maggie Turn it off.

Gary *ignores her and begins to sing all the words.* **Maggie** *folds her arms.*

Gary *begins to sway and dance, doing all he can to attract her attention and make her laugh but she refuses. Avoiding his looks and moving away from him when he gets near her. It becomes a bit outlandish in places.*

Maggie *can stand it no longer and switches off the Bluetooth speaker. Silence.*

Gary I love you, Maggie.

Maggie Once upon a time you could have put anything right with a bunch of red roses. But I'm well past this crap, Gary.

Gary *is stung, genuinely thrown and panicked. He needs a moment to calm himself. Silence.*

Maggie Are you alright?

Gary I don't know whether I'm coming or going, Mag.

Maggie I will always love you, Gary.

Gary You know, you're fucking with my head.

They look at each other for a long time, for as long as you think you can get away with.

Gary D'you mind if I have an emergency vape?

Maggie *nods and* **Gary** *goes to a drawer and takes out a vape.* **Gary** *catches her eye.*

Gary You don't want me to go outside, do you?

She shakes her head and he begins to vape. Trying to compose himself. Silence.

Maggie What's that smell?

Gary It's Chewberry Cosmic Fog.

Maggie What?

Gary Strawberry and passion fruit. I like the tropical flavour.

Its too sickly for **Maggie**. *She takes out some Febreze from the cupboard under the sink and squirts the air around the kitchen.*

She notices the knife on the island, puts down the Febreze and looks at the knife.

Maggie Was this meant for me?

Gary *stops vaping and puts it back in the drawer.*

Gary No. Not you.

Silence.

Maggie Don't be so ridiculous, Gary.

Silence.

Gary I'm lonely. I'm bored. I feel shit about myself.

Maggie I'm sorry.

Silence.

Gary I can't put it eloquent like you. I thought it was just getting older. You're suddenly self-conscious about the years left on the clock. If you're lucky. I'm not happy either, Mag. But I just thought it's middle age.

Maggie Middle age?

Gary Serious.

Maggie Sixty's middle-aged.

Gary Is it?

Maggie We're young . . .

Gary We're not.

Silence.

I know I'm simple. I like my time with you. My time with Annabelle. Family time. I like my holidays. I like having a beer up town, I like going fishing, I like going over West Ham. I like a round of golf. I like cooking. You have no idea how much pleasure I was gonna get out of that pork belly at lunchtime. Getting the crackling just right. Watching Dad test it. And Mum twinkling. Giving Annabelle the best bit. And you laughing. And sighing. And shaking your head. At the ludicrousness. Of my small pleasures. But now all I've got in my head is John.

Silence.

I didn't want this.

Maggie Neither did I.

Gary You think you're the only one that's had to compromise?

Maggie I'm sure I'm not.

Gary Well, you're not, babe.

Maggie I know.

Gary I've put up with things.

Maggie I'm sure you have.

She puts the knife in the sink and replaces the Febreze in the cupboard. She looks at **Gary**.

Gary Do you think doing what I do is a piece of piss?

Maggie I know it's not.

Gary The only reason I do what I do is because I can't do nothing else.

Maggie You could do other things.

Gary I couldn't.

Maggie You could if you wanted to.

Gary It's what I'm cut out for. I don't mind saying it. It's the truth. When Joey Jones saw me knocking out man-made leather handbags on Romford Market. And I was just a kid. He said to me when you've done your exams. You're coming up town with me, boy. I don't mind it. I'm a City boy. It's what I am.

Silence.

I was in the Square Mile and I've been on the Wharf for thirty-odd years and I'm tired, Maggie.

Silence.

I say to myself. Another five years and you'll be mortgage free. And Annabelle's school fees and her university money. I'll have it. It will all be set up.

Silence.

But I'm a fraction of the man I was when I went up town. A husk.

Silence.

I used to be the youngest on my desk. Now it's like 'What's that dozy old Tuesday' still doing here.

Silence.

They roll out the putting mat on a Friday afternoon. Right in the middle of the office.

And there's a monkey bet on this. And a double monkey bet on that. And it's, 'Come on, Gary, liven up. Come on, Gary, join in. Come on, Gary, put your hand in your pocket.'

Silence.

And I'm there sometimes with that putter in my hand. Looking down the mat, looking at the ball. Everyone gathered round. And I'm shaking like a leaf.

Silence.

But you can't show no weakness. Not even a flicker.

Silence.

You've no idea what it's been like. What it's like.
The stress.

Silence.

I've been living on my nerves.

Silence.

You think I want to be out three nights a week? With those wankers. Frankly.

Silence.

Maggie Then pack in.

Gary I can't.

Silence.

Maggie You could do something else you enjoyed.

Gary There's plenty of things I'd enjoy . . .

Maggie Then go for it. Now . . .

Gary But there ain't none of them pays like I get paid now, Mag, and you know it . . .

Maggie I didn't want all this . . . It's ridiculous we're spending all that money sending Annabelle to a prep school . . .

Gary I don't want nothing but the best for her . . .

Silence.

Maggie We don't need a six-bedroom house on the Mount. We never have.

Gary But what about what I want?

Maggie You earn fantastic money. And yet we've got a great big mortgage round our necks. And we're still up against it. And for what? I never wanted this.

Silence.

Gary I always dreamed we'd have three or four kids . . .

Maggie But it's just us, Gary.

Silence.

Gary Well, we've got enough room for everyone to come at Christmas.

Maggie We've been in here for seven years and we've never had everyone for Christmas.

Gary Well, I can't help it if my lot and your lot don't click.

Maggie Okay, Gary.

Silence.

Gary I don't mean this as an insult. I really don't. But the trouble with you, Maggie, is you've never had to scratch around for a few quid.

Silence.

You try growing up with a dad on the bins and a mum who works in Iceland. You try growing up without a tanner in your pocket. With a house that's always a state. Cos no one ain't got no money to fix nothing. Or do nothing.

You try sharing a bedroom with your brother till you're eighteen. You go to a school where no one don't care about learning nothing. They don't care about nothing. Except bunking off and sniffing glue. You try it. Because if you did you might understand why I am the way I am.

Silence.

You was lucky.

Maggie I know.

Gary You had a nice house in Gidea Park.

Maggie It wasn't flash.

Gary You went to a good school.

Maggie And I'm glad I did.

Gary We grew up two mile away from each other. But it might as well have been a different planet.

Maggie Put the violin away, Gary, it doesn't suit you.

Gary Why have your family always looked down on me?

Silence.

Maggie They don't, they love you.

Gary They love me, and they look down on me.

Maggie They don't.

Gary Be honest. They find me crass. They find my taste naff. When I told your mum I was thinking of buying us a villa in Fuengirola, she looked like I'd had a Jimmy Riddle in her lapsang souchong.

Silence.

Your dad's the washing machine and appliance man out of Cambridge Heath Road. And your nan had the bakers on Devons Road. Since when did your lot get to walk about like their shit don't stink?

Maggie My mum and dad worked hard and did well for themselves.

Gary I know they did.

Silence.

Maggie I'm proud of my dad and the way he built his business. I'm proud of the way my mum worked her way up for the NatWest.

Gary Don't you think I'm proud of my mum and dad?

Maggie Well, they've not exactly done very much.

Silence.

Gary They survived.

Silence.

They didn't have a pot to piss in. And they brought up three kids. All doing alright. All of us. They bought our house off the council in 1983 and twenty-five years later they paid off their mortgage. I don't know how they did it. When you're standing where I'm standing. It's a miracle they managed. Don't look down your nose at my family. Don't you dare.

Maggie I don't. I love them.

Silence.

Gary What have I done so wrong?

Maggie What?

Gary In your mum and dad's eyes.

Maggie You haven't done anything wrong.

Gary When all I've done is provide for you. And Annabelle. And give you everything you want.

Silence.

Maggie They don't like the way you spoil Annabelle.

Silence.

And neither do I.

Gary I don't spoil her.

Maggie You do, Gary.

Gary I don't understand why everything has to be so Victorian?

Maggie It doesn't.

Gary She's a kid.

Maggie And she needs boundaries.

Gary She's eight.

Maggie She needs to appreciate the value of things.

Gary She's eight, she's not eighteen.

Maggie I feel like she's growing up easy come, easy go . . .

Gary She's not.

Maggie And because I'm the one that always says no. That has always said no. It can be really horrible. It is really horrible for me. You don't support me . . .

Gary When Annabelle's out of order I support you.

Maggie When she bites me.

Silence.

When she kicks me.

Silence.

When she pulls my hair and screams. Then you support me. But what's the point of me ever saying no? When you arrive on the scene and it's. Yes, Annabelle, whatevs, Annabelle.

Silence.

Sometimes she looks at me and I'm convinced she hates me. She looks at me as if I'm shit. Like I am an actual piece of shit.

Gary She doesn't.

Maggie She does.

Gary She doesn't, babe.

Maggie She does.

Gary You're her mum.

Maggie I know she loves me.

Gary She adores you.

Maggie But she hates me. Just as much. Because I say no. I say no on the school run. I say no after kids' club. I say no after football. I say no before dancing. I say no. Not until you've done your piano practice. I say no at dinner time.

Not until you've done your homework. I say no about the telly, about her iPad, about her Xbox, about sleepovers, about what she'll wear and what she won't wear.

Silence.

Maggie You have no idea how much I resent you for it, Gary. You've reduced my relationship with my daughter to being the person who says no. Because you can't be arsed. You want the easy option.

Silence.

Gary I want her to have nice things. All the things I never had . . .

Maggie You buy her whatever she wants. She doesn't even have to wait for her birthday or Christmas!

Gary You're exaggerating!

Maggie I want you to support me. I want you to say no.

Silence.

I know you've already been talking to her about getting a phone . . .

Gary I swear I haven't . . .

Maggie You have, Gary, she's eight . . .

Gary Well, I've told her she's not having a phone until she goes to big school. I told her when we was at Bluewater. It ain't happening, babe. Move away from the area of Vodafone.

Silence.

I know I can be a better dad. I know I can be a better husband. I know I can.

Maggie It's too late.

Silence.

Gary And what about what I want?

Maggie Like what, Gary?

Gary Like the support I need.

Maggie What support?

Silence.

Gary Well, what do you think?

Maggie I'm not a mind-reader, Gary.

Gary In life. You never ask me how I am.

Maggie Yes I do.

Gary You don't, Maggie. You just think, he's alright. It's obvious. Gary, he's alright. He's always alright. Plods along.

Silence.

Maggie I don't.

Gary When was the last time you asked me how I am?

Silence.

Maggie I asked you earlier.

Gary In a normal setting.

Silence.

Maggie I asked you how you were when you came in on Friday . . .

Gary No you didn't . . .

Maggie I'm sure I did, I'm sure I said, 'How are you? How was your day?'

Gary You didn't, I remember exactly what you said . . .

Maggie Are you going to quibble over words?

Gary You said, 'Do you fancy a Chinese? Because I quite fancy a king prawn with cashew nuts.'

Maggie That's not all I said . . .

Gary No. And then after half an hour going through the menu. Humming and ah-ing. You decided you wanted an Indian!

Maggie What can I say? I'm a woman, I'm fickle.

Gary And then when it come. You didn't eat hardly anything. And you didn't say much either.

Maggie Well, now you know why.

Silence.

Gary You never ask me about work. You avoid talking about my family.

Maggie I don't.

Gary You do. You do, Mag. We both know.

Silence.

You take no interest in me. You just think, 'Gary, he's alright.'

Maggie Well, you hardly take an interest in me.

Silence.

Gary I've wanted us to be close.

Maggie So have I.

Gary I've missed you so much.

Silence.

Maggie I don't know what good this is doing.

Gary I don't understand why you just let things dwindle . . .

Maggie What?

Gary In our sex life.

Silence.

I know a woman has her time. In the month. That's just life. But apart from that time. You know. We was always a once in the week, once at the weekend couple.

Maggie To begin with. Literally years ago. We had Annabelle. You're always out, Gary.

Gary I'm not out five nights a week. I'm not out all weekend.

Silence.

I know all those years. Trying for Annabelle. Fucking hell, sex when you're trying for a baby. As a bloke you spend years of your life dreaming of being with a woman. Who wants you to give her one every day of the week. And not only that. Puts it in your diary so you can look forward to it!

Silence.

I tell you what. If I had to have double pie, double mash and liquor six days in a row, I'd go off of it. And double pie, double mash and liquor is my death-row meal.

Maggie Double pie, double mash and liquor?

Gary Yes, babe.

Maggie It's not necessarily an analogy that would've sprung to my mind.

Silence.

Gary We all know what it's like when you've got a baby. There's a sexual desert and we're all travelling through it. In search of water. Sexy water. But there's nothing as far as the eye can see. Just the odd dune. Maybe a nomad. You're on your camel. I'm on my camel. And then! An oasis! It's Wednesday morning and you're both awake before the alarm's gone off! And the baby's still asleep. And I look at you and you look at me. And my hand goes up your back. And you hook your leg over And hell's bells, Annabelle's awake and she's screaming the house down. We all know.

Maggie *laughs, really laughs.* **Gary** *smiles. They become self-conscious. Silence.*

Gary You're right. Annabelle never gets up in the night. I wanted more.

Maggie What d'you mean?

Gary I wanted more.

Maggie More sex?

Silence.

Gary You just want it over with. I'm just trying to do what you want.

Silence.

We did used to have sexy sex. Didn't we?

Maggie I thought we did.

Gary I haven't stopped being a man. I needed you. I wanted us to try things. To get things going. I wanted us to be connected.

Maggie Try things?

Gary Yeah?

Maggie What sort of things? Not kinky things?

Silence.

Gary You know . . . Whatever you fancy. 'Hello, Mrs Maggie, I'm your friendly gas fitter here to clean your pipes. Oh dear! What's that inside my tool bag? I must have put a nine-inch dildo in there by mistake. What a palaver!'

Maggie Do you honestly think that's what I want?

Gary I don't know what you want. Can't you see I'm clutching at straws here, babe?

Silence.

Maggie I've just gone off it.

Gary What?

Maggie You know what.

Silence.

Gary But don't you want to try?

Maggie I tried last weekend. And it made me feel like shit.

Silence.

Gary I know you think no one looks twice at him. But you're not the only one who can still turn a head on occasion.

Silence.

Maggie You're not having an affair are you, Gary?

She is horrified and involuntarily puts her hands across her chest as if to protect her heart. Silence.

Gary No I'm not. But if Veronica in finance had her way I'd be doing more than taking down my receipts once a week.

Maggie Who the hell is this Veronica?

She wants to cry but won't. Silence.

Gary *and* **Maggie** *look at each other. Silence.*

Maggie Is this it? Is this what we've become?

Gary Maggie, listen to me.

Maggie Maggie? Now I know I'm in trouble . . .

Silence.

Gary Mag, listen to me.

Maggie I'm sorry I'm just upset . . .

She really wants to cry hard again but resists it with all her might.

Gary *goes to her, wanting to comfort her.*

Maggie No, Gary.

Gary I need a hug. I need comfort. Don't you think I need that?

Silence.

You're leaving me.

Silence.

Maggie If I was leaving you I would have said.

Silence.

Maggie I did talk to John about leaving you.

Gary Did you?

Maggie I did.

Silence.

Gary What did he say?

Maggie He said it's too soon.

Gary Did he?

Maggie Yeah.

Gary I must say, I am surprised.

Silence.

Maggie He said, 'We've both got family responsibilities.'

Gary Right.

Maggie He said the romance died with her a long time ago. But there's still loyalty.

Gary Loyalty?

Maggie And family love.

Gary Family love?

Maggie He said he can't let the carnal feelings . . . He said.

Silence.

He said there's no way he can get into us leaving our partners at the minute. He's very caring is John and his wife's not well. Its not just her overactive thyroid. She can hardly walk what with her knees. And her hammer toe.

Gary Right.

Maggie He's that sort of man. Upright.

Gary Yeah. He sounds like a lovely fella.

Silence.

What are you going to do then, Mag?

Maggie *thinks and takes out her iPhone from her pocket and starts looking at it. Scrolling. Silence.*

Gary *retrieves his iPhone and starts looking at his. Scrolling. Silence.*

They scroll in silence for as long as you think you can get away with.

Gary Boutros Boutros-Ghali. Great name.

Maggie What?

Gary Died on Monday. It's on my BBC News app. Boris is coming out for Vote Leave.

Maggie I know you read the news, Gary. I know you read the odd book.

She goes back to her iPhone and so does **Gary**. *Silence.*

Gary What are you gonna do then, Mag?

Silence.

Maggie I thought I could go in one of the guest rooms.

Gary Right.

Maggie For a while.

Gary Right.

Maggie Until we've worked out what we're going to do.

Gary So what is it exactly you're trying to work out, babe?

Silence.

Maggie I thought we could have a period of reflection.

Gary A period of reflection?

Maggie I read an article on the internet.

Gary Right.

Maggie A period of calm reflection.

Gary Calm reflection?

Maggie Yeah.

Gary So what? Are we still having dinner together? And doing things with Annabelle together?

Maggie Yes.

Gary But you're in your own room?

Maggie Or if you want to. You can go in one of the spare rooms . . .

Gary D'you want me to go in one of the spare rooms?

Maggie Only if you want to.

Gary I don't know.

Maggie I mean it would make more sense.

Gary What would?

Maggie Most of the clothes and shoes and everything in our room is my stuff.

Gary What are we going to tell Annabelle?

Maggie I don't know.

She gets upset, holds it in. Silence.

Can we still be friends?

Gary I don't think they do conscious uncoupling in Essex. Unconscious coupling, yep. But not the other way round.

Maggie *laughs, wants to cry, doesn't. Silence.*

Gary And where does John sit in this? In this period of calm reflection. I'll tell you what for nothing. Not in the fucking garage manhandling my golf clubs.

Silence.

Maggie I want to keep in touch with him.

Gary Right.

Maggie I want to see him.

Gary Right.

Maggie I won't go to bed with him. I promise you.

Silence.

If this is the end. If this is the beginning of the end. Then I want us to do it as well as we can. For us. For Annabelle. For our families.

Gary *gets upset, holds it in. Silence.*

He looks at her. Silence.

Gary What do you want, Maggie?

Maggie I don't even know any more . . .

Gary What do you want? What did you want?

Maggie What?

Gary I want to understand you. Please. Let me.

Maggie *nods, thinks. Silence.*

Maggie I think . . . Until I was eighteen. This might seem. Ridiculous. My life was absolutely brilliant. Like there were little disappointments. But life was so content. It was so happy. With mum and dad and my brothers. I loved school. I loved Coopers. All my mates and my teachers. I wasn't very good at sport. I wasn't someone who had lots of boyfriends. I wasn't that bothered. I loved my mates. And I knew blokes fancied me. So it was alright. I didn't care. It didn't matter.

Silence.

In the sixth form I really wanted a VW Beetle. And the summer before uni I learned to drive. I thought I've got to pass my test before I go to Exeter. I have to. I did. And I noticed about a week after I got my A-Level results. About a fortnight before my nineteenth birthday. I noticed this grey VW Beetle. A bit bashed up. But it was parked around the corner from Mum and Dad's. On the corner of Heaton Grange Road. And I thought Mum and Dad have got me it for my birthday. For when I go to uni.

Silence.

And every day I walked past it. Like I had a summer job in Boots in Romford. And every day I went out of my way to go past it. On my way to work. To check was still there.

And I day-dreamed.

Silence.

I counted down the days until my birthday. I imagined driving it down the M4 to uni. Full of all my stuff. I was thinking about seeing it out of the window of my room in halls. I never parked it under a tree. I was already planning my days down at the beach at Exmouth.

Silence.

You've no idea the things I thought of walking past this car every day. Out of my way. On my way to work at Boots. My imagination was out of control. You have no idea what my imagination could be like. I've never wanted anything more in my entire life than that car. Neither before nor since. It sounds ridiculous but it's true.

Silence.

Anyway, the day of my birthday came. And I looked at the presents from my brothers. And Mum and Dad. And I saw it. I couldn't take my eyes off it. There was a little square box. That Mum and Dad said I should save until last. It was the keys. It was the keys.

Silence.

And I opened the little box. And there was a beautiful ring. You remember it? It was a ruby, with diamonds. And Mum had tears in her eyes. 'We knew how much you loved your grandma's ring. Your grandma wouldn't have wanted anyone but you to have it.' And I was up and out and out of the front door. Round the corner into Heaton Grange Road. The car was gone. I walked across the road into Raphael Park. And I raged and howled. I turned myself inside out. No one could fathom it.

Silence.

It was such a knock. Nothing had ever gone wrong before.

Silence.

Dad had sorted me out a car as it goes. Before I went to Exeter. An old Fiesta. Uni was alright. The English degree was alright. I met some alright people. There was a lot of drinking and shagging. And posh boys. Rugby boys. Some of the girls I lived with were gross. Worse than the boys. Nothing about it was bohemian. I should have just left really. But you don't just pack in when you come from a family like mine.

Silence.

I wrote hundreds of letters. To TV companies, film companies, magazines, newspapers, everywhere. Nothing. A mate of a mate of a mate worked with Terry Christian. And arranged a coffee. But he cancelled. I graduated, I was back home. Me and Mum weren't getting on. Uncle William knew someone who had a junior HR position in an insurance firm up town. And there you go. Bosh. Thirty years later.

Silence.

I've counted my blessings for thirty years, Gary. And I feel very lucky to earn a good wage. To have a good job. But I wanted to do something I enjoyed.

Silence.

I did make one friend at uni I kept for a bit. She was doing English with me. Jo. Joanna. She wanted to work in TV like me. She really struggled as well. Did all sorts of jobs.

Temping and waitressing. She was in a shared house down in Turnpike Lane. She kept saying to me. Come and live with me. And I was all geared up to. And then she got this job as a runner for Carlton Television. Remember them? And I couldn't handle it. I was so angry. I was jealous and silly. And I let the friendship go. I let Jo go. But I couldn't let the feeling go. I've never been able to let the feeling go.

Silence.

This isn't what I wanted.

Silence.

We're friends on Facebook. We connected when I had Annabelle. She saw a picture another uni random commented on and . . . And we started to be in touch a bit.

Gary I remember you going to see her.

Maggie Yeah.

Gary You said you had a top afternoon.

Maggie Hmm.

Silence.

There's no direct way to get to Crouch End. It's really annoying. I got the train to Liverpool Street. And walked round to Moorgate. Annabelle was a nightmare.

Got the train back out to Hornsey. I was an hour early. I was so paranoid about getting there. And I thought I can't knock on the door an hour early. So I had a wander round Crouch End.

Silence.

Annabelle perked up. I went in Gail's for a coffee. Had a cinnamon bun. And I started to dream.

Silence.

I was the TV producer. Not Jo.

Silence.

I was looking in the window of this boutique. A street fashion boutique you could say. I caught my reflection in the window. Annabelle holding my hand. And she said to me, 'Mummy, why are you crying?'

Silence.

And I thought pull yourself together, Maggie. You don't want Jo to see you like this. And the more I told myself to pull myself together. That made it even worse. By the time I got to the top of Jo's road I could hardly put one foot in front of the other. And it had started to rain.

And Annabelle was getting in on the act. Grizzling and sniffing and sobbing. And I thought my heartache isn't even my own any more.

Silence.

So we just came home.

Silence.

That was when I started to force the issue of going back to work.

Silence.

Why do people ever see things through? Why do they ever stay? It's so hard.

Silence.

I want a new life, Gary.

Silence.

Gary I had no idea, babe, I . . .

Silence.

Why've you never talked to me like this before?

Maggie I didn't think I could.

Gary Why are you saying that?

Maggie You never seemed interested in me. You only ever seemed interested in Annabelle.

Gary You can talk to me . . .

Maggie I can't, Gary. It's always just banter with you.

Silence.

Gary Everyone's disappointed. Everyone's got regrets. Everyone wonders. That's just what it is to be human. To be a person. And to be alive. Life's hard. Life is hard. And the older you get the harder it gets.

Silence.

To me it's about the little things. They get you through.

He glances at the pork belly on the plate.

Gary Having Mum and Dad round for a roast to say thank you. Everyone having a laugh.

Scrutinising the crackling. Not too pliable. Not too much un-rendered fat. But you don't want to chip your tooth on it.

Silence.

Maggie What did you want, Gary? What do you want? Go on. Tell me. Don't be scared. Say whatever you want.

Silence.

Gary I've got everything I ever wanted.

Maggie You've got everything you ever wanted?

Gary Yeah.

Maggie *is flabbergasted.*

Maggie But what are you going to do with the rest of your life, Gary?

Silence.

Surely there must be things, there must have been things . . .

Gary I would have liked a bigger family. But you know that.

Silence.

You talk like most of our marriage. Twelve, thirteen years of a marriage. Don't count for nothing. Except heartache and pain. Well, I'm not having it, Maggie. It's not just your marriage. It's my marriage. It's not just your life. It's my life.

Silence.

What about our wedding anniversary? Our tenth? Your mum and dad had Annabelle.

And I took you to Venice. Don't you remember before I got out your real present. I gave you baked beans. A tin. Because your tenth, it's tin ain't it? Tin.

He controls his emotion. Silence.

And you looked at that tin of Heinz baked beans. And you looked at me. Right in my eyes. Looked at me. And you said, 'I love you, Gary.' And I knew you loved me like I loved you. And I thought I'm proud of this. I'm proud of us. Ten years. And here's to the next ten. Yeah, we've been together a long time. And we've had our ups and downs. And don't you think there haven't been times when I've felt like jacking it all in? Fine. I could reel off a list of every single brilliant thing we've done. And every moment of happiness and joy we've shared. And we'd be here another two hours and it still wouldn't be enough.

Fine you feel what you feel. You've said what you've said. But don't mug me off with this bullshit that our whole marriage is shit just because you've had your head turned.

Silence.

I've heard what you've said, Mag. Every single word. You know what? You let me take Annabelle in hand from now on. Let me do it. And we're getting a babysitter in once a week now. So we can go out. And if your lot are offended. Or my lot are offended. I'll straighten them out. And I get what you're saying about . . . I get it. I get it.

Silence.

I promise you I won't ask you for no sex. I promise you. I swear. We've got to get things straight . . . You want calm reflection. I will give you calm reflection. If you want me to go in one of the spare rooms I will. I don't mind the one at the back. I'll go in that one. I get it, Mag . . .

Maggie Gary . . .

Gary And you know what? I know I've got to pack in up town. I know I have. It's killing me. You're right. Next thing, you know, I'll drop down dead. There's something else I can do there's bound to be . . . I can re-train. There's something. I'll find something, Mag. You see.

Silence.

And if you want to downsize and move somewhere else. Then we can talk about it. We can. I'm open to ideas, Mag, I am. I promise you I am. If that's what you want. That's what we're doing. If you want move to Crouch End, we can move to Crouch End.

Maggie Changing everything isn't going to change everything any more. Not inside. Not inside . . .

Gary I know, I know . . .

Maggie I'm tired of hoping and dreaming. And waiting and wishing. And telling myself it will all be alright in the end. I'm tired, Gary. I'm tired.

They look at each other for a long time, for as long as you think you can get away with.

Gary Look . . . I'll take Annabelle football. We can put on a nice show for Mum and Dad. They won't stay long. And when Annabelle's gone to bed tonight we can talk. Sensible like.

Maggie Can we?

Gary *finds courage. Silence.*

Gary I've got to be honest about one thing. I've got to be honest about myself. About the sort of fella I am.

Silence.

You saying about keeping seeing John? It's asking too much of me.

Silence.

Fine, you want to try and work out what you want to do. I'm gutted. I'm more devastated by this than you'll ever know, darling. But I'm a big boy. I'll deal with it. And I'll fight for you. I'll fight for my marriage. I'll fight like you've never seen me fight in all my life. But I'm flesh and blood. I'm flesh and blood.

Silence.

If you're going on seeing John then our marriage is as good as over.

Silence.

But, Mag, babe . . . You know what I think? This isn't the end. This isn't the end for us. No way. We've not even got anywhere near the end of the road. This is the middle. This is the middle. This is *The Empire Strikes Back*.

Maggie *The Empire Strikes Back*?

Gary Lando shafts his mates. Han gets frozen in carbonite and Princess Leia's all heartbroken. Luke sacks off his Jedi training. And all these years later, I'm still like. Luke, mate, you can't mug Yoda off . . .

Maggie You want me to give up John?

Gary *nods.* **Maggie** *thinks, gets upset, holds it in. Silence.*

Gary At least give us half a chance, darling.

They look at each other for a long time, for as long as you think you can get away with.

Maggie We're miles apart, Gary, literally miles apart.

Gary Okay, okay.

Maggie I don't know how we can possibly come together?

Gary *thinks, remembers something and heads to a cupboard. He takes out something folded in a brown paper bag. He gives it to* **Maggie**. *She is a bit hesitant.*

Gary It was a little extra for Valentine's. But I forgot to pack it for the weekend.

Maggie *takes out a single Rolo.*

Gary Roses are red, violets are blue, I saved my last Rolo, especially for you.

Maggie *holds everything in.*

Gary You know what I'm like, if I'd not hid it, I'd have definitely eaten it. And that would have sort of. Defeated the object. But like the monumental dickhead I am I ballsed it right up. Anyway, got there in the end.

Silence.

I can't be a completely different person, Mag. I'm nearly fifty years of age. I am what I am. I mean all the things I said. It's not Gary-bants this time, babe. I will do things better.

He finds courage.

I can't completely change your life. Only you can do that. And if that's what you really want then let's call it a day.

He takes in their big kitchen.

I don't care about any of this really. You're all I ever wanted. It's a rut. We're in a massive rut. We'll get through it.

Maggie Will we, though?

Gary *hesitates, silence.*

Gary I think I'm a bit low. I think I've been like it for a long time. For years.

Silence.

It's weird, I thought not wanting anything any more was a sign of contentment. But it's not, is it? It's the opposite. I'm not putting it on you. I know it's down to me. But it takes a lot of bollocks for me to admit it. You know?

Maggie Thank you. Thank you.

Silence.

Gary I feel really old. All of a sudden I feel really old.

Maggie So do I.

Silence.

Gary Annabelle won't be up for another hour. Why don't we have some breakfast? Let's have breakfast . . . Let's just have a nice chilled family Sunday.

Maggie I don't know if I can see anyone today . . .

Gary Don't worry about that, let's just have breakfast.

Maggie *looks at him, uncertain.*

Gary All I want is little bit more time. So I can really show you what I'm made of.

Silence.

I'm sure if this John's a decent fella he'll understand. I'm sure if this John really thinks something of you he'll wait for you.

They look at each other for a long time, for as long as you think you can get away with.

Finally **Maggie** *nods.* **Gary** *nods. He goes to the Bluetooth speaker and puts on the radio. He turns the volume down. Music from Heart radio subtly fills the kitchen.*

Maggie *goes to the cupboard and gets out some muesli.*

She goes to the fridge and gets out some milk. She puts them on the island and goes in search of some bowls and spoons. But she remembers **Gary** *smashed all the bowls.*

Maggie *has an idea and ferrets around in another cupboard. She brings out two of Annabelle's Disney bowls from when she was small.* **Gary** *smiles at the sight of the bowls.*

He looks at the broken glass pane in the sideboard and thinks. He has an idea. He goes to the cupboard **Maggie** *fished out the muesli from and takes out a big box of Frosties. He takes the cereal from the cardboard box and flattens out the cardboard.*

He takes it to the sideboard and holds it up against the frame of the smashed pane in the sideboard. He then gets some scissors from one drawer and some Sellotape from another drawer and cuts the cardboard into a rectangle which will cover over the broken glass pane.

He does it with care. **Maggie** *watches him as he Sellotapes the cardboard into place. He admires his work and looks at* **Maggie**. *They look at each other for a long time, for as long as you think you can get away with.*

Gary *moves and flicks on the kettle and watches it start to re-boil. He takes the teapot and fishes out the teabags from earlier and chucks them in the bin. And then goes to sink and gives it a rinse.*

He looks at the teapot and thinks. He brings it over to the island and draws **Maggie**'*s attention to it.*

Maggie What is it, love?

Gary You see this teapot . . .

Maggie Yeah.

Gary We must always keep this teapot. Whatever happens and wherever we go. It's precious.

Maggie How come?

Gary It survived.

He smiles. **Maggie** *smiles and nods, less certain. The kettle boils.*

Fade.

The End.